How Not to be the Perfect Husband

This is a STAR FIRE book

STAR FIRE
Crabtree Hall, Crabtree Lane
Fulham, London SW6 6TY
United Kingdom

www.star-fire.co.uk

First published 2007

07 09 11 10 08

1 3 5 7 9 10 8 6 4 2

Star Fire is part of The Foundry Creative Media Company Limited

ISBN: 978 1 84451 941 5

Printed in China

Thanks to: Cat Emslie, Andy Frostick, Victoria Lyle,
Sara Robson, Nick Wells

How Not to be the Perfect

Husband

Ulysses Brave

STAR FIRE

Foreword

There are so many rules today, scrupulously compiled by faceless committees of governing and busy bodies. Over the years many people have appealed to me for clarity and purpose on such matters. They say that it is difficult to know how to behave in modern society, so I have penned some careful advice based on simple, old-fashioned common sense.

Ulysses Brave

The good husband loves
to show off to his
wife's friends.

A good husband is always conducting sleep research in front of the TV.

Husbands love to flirt with danger, especially in their own back garden.

*Husbands like to be pampered,
but never admit it.*

Some (former) husbands carry out dangerous PR stunts to campaign for greater legal rights.

Middle-aged husbands often adopt a slick-back look in an attempt to capture the golden years of the rock'n'roll youth they never had.

When children use their
camera phones remember
they will show the playful
pictures of their father to
their friends.

The perfect husband will always
take pleasure in the gift of his
own wind.

A perfect husband will
have difficulty crawling out of
bed in the mornings, especially
if drink has been employed
the night before.

Husbands always try to look natural in family photos, but rarely succeed.

Husbands like to excercise their angry face at least twice a week, generally when being disturbed watching sport on TV.

Husbands like to strike out on their own, but quickly become disillusioned, cold and hungry.

Husbands are always intrigued
by a beautiful new neighbour and
will quickly imagine a series of
hopeful encounters.

If someone disturbs his
sneaky rest, a good husband
will always pretend he has been
roused from a deep sleep.

Husbands often practice making a bad smell and pretending that it is not their own.

The alert husband will pretend to be exhausted when asked to read a bed-time story to the children.

A foolish grin can work wonders
for a guilty husband.

A husband will always make a disproportionate fuss about toothache. The perfect wife will resist any comparisons with the pain of childbirth.

Husbands will take simple exercise as little as possible.

Husbands like to think of themselves as hunter-gatherers, but are always relieved to come home to a pre-packed supermarket-sourced supper.

Husbands expect boundless sympathy for self-induced pain or humiliation.

A good husband will rarely go out of his depth, except in the daily interactions with family, friends and work colleagues.

Lost? Of course he's not lost. The true husband will never quit and never, ever, ask directions from a local.

If a wife becomes angry with her husband he will try to calm her down by staring blankly at her.

Husbands like to undertake manly tasks and will spend hours practising in front of the children.

A husband will do anything to get out of the washing up, from hurting his finger on a piece of paper, to drowning in a nearby lake.

The perfect husband will always take the longest possible route to completing a simple task.

A good husband is neither venal, nor lazy, but is often very worn down by the heroic responsibilities of his life.

Rule No. 22.
Some husbands can be cute.

Rule No. 23.
Not yours.

Husbands specialize in making leaps in the dark, anticipating admiration for their courage in the face of ignorance.

Pointless trials of strength are a speciality for many husbands.

Husbands do not like to be
woken up in the mornings by
their children. Most husbands
will assume that their wife
will be ready to deal with
any such irritation.

When in a tight spot, do not ask for advice.

Come back soon!